THE SHARK IS BROKEN

BY IAN SHAW AND JOSEPH NIXON

MUSIC AND THIRD-PARTY MATERIALS USE NOTE

Licensees are solely responsible for obtaining formal written permission from copyright owners to use copyrighted music and/or other copyrighted third-party materials (e.g. artworks, logos) in the performance of this play and are strongly cautioned to do so. If no such permission is obtained by the licensee, then the licensee must use only original music and materials that the licensee owns and controls. Licensees are solely responsible and liable for clearances of all third-party copyrighted materials, including without limitation music, and shall indemnify the copyright owners of the play(s) and their licensing agent, Dramatists Play Service, an imprint of Concord Theatricals Corp., against any costs, expenses, losses and liabilities arising from the use of such copyrighted third-party materials by licensees. For music, please contact the appropriate music licensing authority in your territory for the rights to any incidental music.

IMPORTANT BILLING AND CREDIT REQUIREMENTS

If you have obtained performance rights to this title, please refer to your licensing agreement for important billing and credit requirements.

THE SHARK IS BROKEN premiered at the Rialto Theatre in Brighton, England, on July 24, 2019, and then transferred to Assembly George Square Studios on August 2, 2019. It was directed by Guy Masterson and the cast was as follows:

RICHARD DREYFUSS .... Liam Murray Scott
ROY SCHEIDER .... Duncan Henderson
ROBERT SHAW .... Ian Shaw

The original West End production of THE SHARK IS BROKEN was produced by Sonia Friedman Productions, Scott Landis, GFour Productions, Larry Magid, and Tulchin Bartner Productions, in association with Jane Bergère, at the Ambassadors Theatre in London, England, on October 9, 2021. Subsequently, it played the Royal Alexandra Theatre in Toronto, Canada, opening on September 30, 2022. It was directed by Guy Masterson and the cast was as follows:

RICHARD DREYFUSS .... Liam Murray Scott
ROY SCHEIDER .... Demetri Goritsas
ROBERT SHAW .... Ian Shaw

The original Broadway production of THE SHARK IS BROKEN was produced by Sonia Friedman Productions, Scott Landis, GFour Productions, Tulchin Bartner Productions, Eilene Davidson Productions, LD Entertainment, No Guarantees, Jane Bergère, Richard Batchelder, Larry Magid, Theatre Tours International Ltd, Shooting the Breeze, Cue to Cue Productions/James deRoy, Marc Goldman/Richard & Claudia Beeny, Jill Lenhart/Yara Shoemaker Couture, Moellenberg/Hornos, Pinnacle Productions/Bill Hanney, and Jesse Singer/Matthew Levy, at the John Golden Theatre on August 10, 2023. It was directed by Guy Masterson, the scenic and costume designs were by Duncan Henderson, the lighting design was by Jon Clark, the sound design and original music were by Adam Cork, the projection design was by Nina Dunn for PixelLux, wig design and construction was by Campbell Young Associates, and the production stage manager was Timothy R. Semon. The cast was as follows:

RICHARD DREYFUSS .... Alex Brightman
ROY SCHEIDER .... Colin Donnell
ROBERT SHAW .... Ian Shaw

CHARACTERS

RICHARD DREYFUSS

ROY SCHEIDER

ROBERT SHAW

PLACE

On board the *Orca*, on the open ocean east of Martha's Vineyard,
between East Chop and Oak Bluffs.

THE SHARK IS BROKEN

Scene 1

Darkness. SFX: Ominous theme music, which descends into sounds of a mechanical shark breaking down.

Lights up.

Roy Scheider sits at the table to read his New York Times.

SFX: Launch approaches and bumps the Orca.

Richard Dreyfuss appears and enters.

DREYFUSS. What a god almighty fucking waste of time!

SCHEIDER. Jesus! What's eating you now?

DREYFUSS. The title character has had a cardiac infarction. Bruce is dead!

SCHEIDER. Well, at least it's consistent. They'll just get another one from the boat shed.

DREYFUSS. How many of those things they got, anyway? Three? Four? We've been on this boat, what, five days? None of them fucking work. This whole thing is a disaster.

Dreyfuss grabs the heater and tries to turn it on.

Christ, it's cold. Is this thing working?

SCHEIDER. Let me try.

Scheider turns it on easily.

That should do it.

SFX: Muffled shouting—splash.

What are they doing to it?

DREYFUSS. Don't ask me, man. Why does it take so goddamn long?

SCHEIDER. Well…it's not the time it takes to take the take that takes the time… It's the time it takes between the takes that takes the time to take the take.

> *Beat.*

DREYFUSS. How much time did that take you?

Why are the goddamn things so unreliable? They can put a man on the moon but they can't make a mechanical fish that floats?

SCHEIDER. I was talking with Bob, and as I understand it it's to do with the dynamics of the mechanism. You see, Bruce is powered with pneumatics, right, rather than hydraulics? Because oil and water don't mix.

DREYFUSS. Right.

SCHEIDER. Well, Bruce is designed to be a neutral weight, so he'll float, but pneumatics use compressed air, and the compressed air causes fluctuations in weight. So the longer he's out there and the more he moves the heavier he gets.

DREYFUSS. That's fascinating, Roy. You know, it makes me think it would have been easier to just get a real shark.

SCHEIDER. You serious?

DREYFUSS. Sure, why not? Get a tame shark. How hard can it be?

SCHEIDER. You ever seen a real live shark?

DREYFUSS. I'm from Queens, man! Of course I've never seen a real live shark!

SCHEIDER. Richard, you cannot tame a shark.

DREYFUSS. No?

SCHEIDER. No. Whattya gonna do? He eats someone he gets a tap on the nose, he doesn't eat someone you give him a cookie?

Anyway, the weather guy said there's a warm front moving in. Plenty of sunshine; maybe we can catch a few rays.

DREYFUSS. Yeah? I look to you like the kind of guy who likes to catch a few rays? My skin bypasses "tan" and goes directly to "sunstroke."

SCHEIDER. Hey don't knock it, Richard. It lowers your blood pressure, lifts your mood, gives you vitamin D…

Pause.

DREYFUSS. Is this the way you saw your career panning out? My first picture was *Valley of the Dolls*.

SCHEIDER. Who were you in it?

DREYFUSS. Ach, I'm in it for all of forty-five seconds. One line. Just an extra really. What was your first one?

SCHEIDER. A little Oscar winner you may have heard of called *The Curse of the Living Corpse*.

DREYFUSS. Really?

SCHEIDER. Not exactly Shakespeare, huh?

DREYFUSS. No.

Pause.

You've done Shakespeare, right, Roy?

SCHEIDER. Sure—*Romeo and Juliet*, New York Shakespeare Festival. I was Mercutio.

DREYFUSS. Yeah, I'm gonna do Shakespeare some day. I just can't decide which role I'd be best suited to. Hamlet or Prince Hal?… Hey, you know Robert works all the time with Harold Pinter? I'm gonna ask him to hook me up. Jesus, I never thought I'd miss West Hollywood… That's where I should be, instead of freezing my balls off here. But I guess the film wouldn't work without me.

SCHEIDER. Come again?

DREYFUSS. Hooper's the brains of the operation, the scientist, the rationalist; without him there's no shark hunt! No movie!

SCHEIDER. Well that's one way of looking at it.

DREYFUSS. D'you read the book?

SCHEIDER. Um, yeah.

DREYFUSS. You did? They told me not to read it, said it might confuse me. So…what's it like?

SCHEIDER. Well it's no *Great Gatsby*.

DREYFUSS. Okay.

SCHEIDER. But you know what they say. It's easier to make a good movie out of a bad book than out of a great book.

DREYFUSS. Is that so?

SCHEIDER. I don't know, I mean he…Steven…changed a lot of things for the script.

DREYFUSS. Yeah?

SCHEIDER. Yeah, uh, for example, in the book Hooper is having an affair with Brody's wife.

DREYFUSS. He is? …Damn!

> *Beat.*

SCHEIDER. What do you think of Steven?

DREYFUSS. Well he's, I mean, the first thing is I think people underestimate him. He may be just a kid, but he's, you know, he's an old head on young shoulders… Having said that…I think he may be clinically insane!

SCHEIDER. Really?

DREYFUSS. Yeah! He's shooting on the ocean. Nobody shoots on the ocean! You know how many water tanks Universal has? I mean, you know what it's like man, you work your butt off, you're at the mercy of nature—wind, rain, tides, sun—overexposure to all of them. Jews should stay away from water. Nothing good ever happened to any Jew on the water.

SCHEIDER. Didn't Jesus walk on water?

DREYFUSS. Yeah! …And look what happened to him!

> *Beat.*

I mean, call me old-fashioned, but I think when you're making a four-million-dollar studio picture you should have a script. It seems to me that we talk about something over dinner and the next day it's in the scene Gottlieb hands us! You can't make big-budget Hollywood movies on the fly, man.

SCHEIDER. Somebody…uh, one of the crew…told me that we're already two million dollars over budget.

DREYFUSS. Who told you that? Was it Tom? Sure feels like it's true, and we still got all of the shark stuff to shoot. If the fucking thing ever starts working that is. Otherwise we're going to be in *Planet of the Apes* without the monkeys, man!

SCHEIDER. If this is going to be such a turkey, why did you sign up?

DREYFUSS. Oh, *(Laughs.)* I fucked up, is what happened. I shot this thing last year—*The Apprenticeship of Duddy Kravitz*…serious drama, and I thought "This is it, baby, this is the big time. This is gonna make you a star!" but…I saw the premiere up in Montreal and, fuck, man I stink in it.

But I was the same with *American Graffiti.* So I'm watching the rough cut, right?—I go clammy cold. All of a sudden, I'm seeing me…and I'm shaped like Smokey the Bear, and I've got this awful monotonal, nasal voice and I'm the worst, right? George Lucas sees me and says "What do you think?" and I say "Well, George, it's a nice movie…and I've already figured out how you can cut me out." Lucas told me I was crazy.

SCHEIDER. You were terrific. It's a great movie. You know, when I signed, Dick let slip that the studio wanted Charlton Heston for Brody!

DREYFUSS. Yeah? Well, you know who they wanted for Hooper? Jon Voight—you know, that big, blond son of a bitch. How the hell did they end up with us?

SCHEIDER. Maybe Steven doesn't like big stars.

DREYFUSS. Doesn't like big stars? Why the hell not?

SCHEIDER. I don't know, but I would guess for reasons of realism.

DREYFUSS. Realism? They got a shark out there the size of a truck and they're worried about realism?!

SCHEIDER. Well maybe this is a new kind of movie. I mean, you saw *2001*, right? The Kubrick film? No big names in that.

DREYFUSS. Yeah! That movie made absolutely no sense whatsoever.

SCHEIDER. You know, Robert told me that Kubrick offered him a lead role in it.

DREYFUSS. Really? What, one of the astronauts?

SCHEIDER. No. Actually he wanted him to play the lead monkey…

DREYFUSS. Hahahaha! Wait, really?

SCHEIDER. Robert turned him down. He said "You're not going to make a monkey out of me!"

DREYFUSS. Man, that is perfect casting! Shaw the ape-man. The Neanderthal!… This fucking weather! Ah, I hate this place. Fucking New England. People look at me like they've never seen a Jew before.

SCHEIDER. I'd say it's a distinct possibility that they haven't.

SFX: A launch strikes the boat.

Shaw appears.

DREYFUSS. I feel like I'm in the goddamn zoo. I'm out of place here, man. This is not Queens.

SCHEIDER. No, it's not.

DREYFUSS. The people here are a bunch of white, Protestant, Lutheran, stick-up-butt, bridge-playing, clam-chowder-eating shitheads!

Shaw enters carrying a pack of cigarettes for Scheider, which he throws to him, and a book.

SHAW. Ladies. You're sick of that clam chowder too?

DREYFUSS. God, yes! How long have we been shooting? Seven weeks?

SCHEIDER. Eight!

DREYFUSS. I get away from here, I'm not going to touch seafood for the next twenty years, man.

SHAW. Christ, what I wouldn't do for a simple plate of devilled kidneys on toast.

DREYFUSS. I've no idea what the fuck that is, but it sounds disgusting.

SHAW. You're a philistine, boy!

SCHEIDER. Did you have any trouble getting to set, Robert? My driver went via the Edgartown Vineyard Haven Road but the traffic was terrible so then we dropped down to the Edgartown West Tisbury Road…

SHAW. Roy, stop! You're talking about roads again! If I have any trouble getting to sleep tonight you can come over to mine and tell me all about it.

Shaw opens his book. Pause.

DREYFUSS. *(To Shaw.)* What are you reading?

SHAW. Damon Runyon.

DREYFUSS. Who's that?

SHAW. Christ, the lights are on but nobody's home. One of your compatriots, but far superior.

SCHEIDER. Richard, you must have heard of Damon Runyon.

DREYFUSS. Must I? You can't expect me to know everything.

SHAW. I think our mistake is expecting you to know anything.

>*Pause.*

DREYFUSS. So Roy, what does the *Times* have to say about Nixon today?

>*Scheider finds the page.*

SCHEIDER. "Almost forgotten, by the time Mr. Nixon tendered his resignation, were his days of glory only two years ago, when he began dismantling the cold war that had dominated American politics for a quarter century, with his dramatic journeys to Peking and Moscow and the signing of the first limitation on the deadly nuclear arms race. Almost forgotten were his successes in ending American involvement in the bitterly divisive Vietnam War and in halting the draft. Gone was the sweeping mandate Mr. Nixon had won from the American electorate in November, 1972, when he carried forty-nine states (all but Massachusetts plus the District of Columbia)—with the help of what he liked to call *(Imitating Nixon.)* 'The silent majority'—the middle-class Americans of the suburbs and small towns and farms. Gone were the dreams of an historic realignment that would make the Republicans the majority party by stripping blue-collar workers and Southerners from Franklin D. Roosevelt's coalition."

SHAW. *(Imitating Nixon.)* I am not a crook!

DREYFUSS. Jesus, that makes him sound like a saint. Fuck him!

SHAW. The man appalls me, but I can't help feeling some curious sort of pity for him.

DREYFUSS. You pity him? Why?

SHAW. I think he hates himself.

SCHEIDER. What a president! Christ! Well there's one thing to be said for all this…there will never be a more immoral president than Tricky Dicky.

DREYFUSS. Hey, you know who kind of looks like Nixon? Murray.

SHAW. Hahaha! He does! I wonder if that's why Steven cast him as the mayor?

> *SFX: Shark-repair noises from shore.*

SCHEIDER. Do you know what they're doing to it?

SHAW. According to the lad Joyner, the damn fool contraption has salt water in its workings. It's going to take at least an hour to hoist it out of the brine and drain it.

SCHEIDER. I think we've underestimated the power of the sea.

SHAW. Yes lads—we have angered Neptune.

DREYFUSS. I think you mean Poseidon.

SHAW. Christ, what did they teach you at school? They're the same bloody god!

DREYFUSS. Oh, shit. I knew that. What, you think I'm an idiot?

SHAW. I presume that's a rhetorical question.

SCHEIDER. Oh by the way, Robert, here's the latest version of the Indianapolis speech.

SHAW. D'you read it?

SCHEIDER. Uhhh, yeah.

SHAW. *(Reading.)* By Christ there's some stinky writing here! And it's five pages long! We're not doing a bloody play!

SCHEIDER. I'm not sure even Olivier could make it work! They might have to cut it.

SHAW. They can't cut it—it's the heart of the film. It explains why Quint's a fucking maniac.

DREYFUSS. Robert, listen…I er…I haven't had the chance to tell you how much I loved your Claudius. It was… You were the best Claudius I've ever seen… Do you think I could do Shakespeare?

> *Pause while Shaw takes a good look at Dreyfuss, summing him up.*

SHAW. …No!!

> *Beat.*

DREYFUSS. Are we going to be here for the rest of our lives?

SHAW. I hope to god not! What a godforsaken place. Have either of you noticed certain facial features keep cropping up with the locals round here? There's a nose and a jawline that I keep seeing again and again.

SCHEIDER. Now that you mention it…

SHAW. I don't suppose there's much else to do here in the winter months. Might as well cuddle up with your sister!

> *Dreyfuss makes the sound of a banjo, like the musical duel in* Deliverance.

SCHEIDER. Did you know Bob built the squid in *20,000 Leagues Under the Sea*?

SHAW. I did know that. The technicians are wonderful.

DREYFUSS. We should have shot it in a goddamn tank! It's gruelling and pointless!

SHAW. It wouldn't look the same in a tank. The story's important, the shark's important, but the sea is crucial. I wouldn't have taken the job if we were shooting in a bloody tank. You think you're working too hard, do you? You think you're overstretched? You Beverly Hills milk puff! Well, do you?

DREYFUSS. I think I'm pretty much busting my balls, yes.

SHAW. Good god! When they call wrap and take us in speedboats back to the local bar and you drape yourself in a blonde or—what was it last night? A brunette—what do you think the crew are doing? Those poor bastards have been freezing their arses off in the water half the time, and then they have to clean and maintain the cameras, reweld, repatch, and all the other lugging, striking, and general shit that we never see—why do you think we're first at the bar? Mike has to balance the camera on his shoulders and flex his legs to keep the dancing horizon steady in shot—do you know how physically demanding that is? If you punched his torso, you'd break your little TV actor's hand. The divers' fingers are cut to pieces by the barnacles—and you sit there whining like a fucking baby!

DREYFUSS. Jesus, you are a vindictive motherfucker, you know that?

SCHEIDER. Fellas, if we really are going to be here for the rest of our lives, let's try to make the best of it.

> *Shaw sighs.*

SHAW. Still, it will be worth it in the end, I s'pose.

DREYFUSS. What, you think this is going to be a hit?

SHAW. The best films I've been in have made no money, and the worst have made a fortune.

SCHEIDER. And which category do we fit into?

SHAW. Well, let me put it like this. I offered my whole salary plus the overage for a percentage of the profits. Zanuck and Brown turned me down.

SCHEIDER. So it's going to be terrible but make a bundle?

SHAW. What do you think? Do you imagine it's going to be a second *Citizen Kane*? Bread and circuses, chums. I pray this is as simpleminded as Hollywood films ever get.

SCHEIDER. Cinema for "the people" then?

SHAW. The lowest common denominator, Roy.

DREYFUSS. Interesting…

> *Beat.*

SHAW. What?

DREYFUSS. I'd heard that you were a "socialist"?

SHAW. What did you say?

DREYFUSS. I'd be interested to learn how you square your "left-wing principles" with the large sums of money you make. I mean, presumably you donate your entire wages to the workers.

SHAW. You little turd, in England they tax you ninety percent!

DREYFUSS. So that's why you live in Ireland!

> *Shaw pulls out a knife… Dreyfuss is seriously alarmed…*
> *Then Shaw reaches into a pocket and brings out an apple…*
> *He slowly cuts a piece off and pops it in his mouth.*

SHAW. An apple a day…

DREYFUSS. What?

SHAW. Keeps the doctor away. That's what they used to say. You could do with a few of these, boy. And some exercise. You're in terrible shape for a man your age. It's a tragedy.

DREYFUSS. Now, wait a minute!

SHAW. A little man like you can't carry that amount of fat. You're a disgrace! I bet you couldn't even do ten press-ups.

DREYFUSS. What is this, West Point?

SHAW. Or even five! I'll give you a hundred dollars right now if you can do five press-ups.

> *Shaw plants his knife into the table to cement the bet.*

DREYFUSS. A hundred dollars? Alright!

SCHEIDER. Richard…

DREYFUSS. No, if he wants to see press-ups I'll give him press-ups. And they're called push-ups.

SHAW. Go on then, we're waiting!

DREYFUSS. Okay.

> *Dreyfuss gets down on the floor and does a push-up.*

One!

SHAW. Back straight. No cheating!

> *Dreyfuss starts again. Shaw retrieves a half bottle of bourbon from the cool box and takes a swig from it.*

DREYFUSS. Two!

SHAW. D'you know how much money I have to make to look after my family?

DREYFUSS. Three!

SHAW. A simple trip to a McDonald's restaurant in Los Angeles cost me fifty dollars! Then there's school fees…

DREYFUSS. Four!

> *Dreyfuss collapses. Shaw laughs heartily.*

SCHEIDER. Fifty dollars at McDonald's? How many kids do you have?

SHAW. Nine…so far.

SCHEIDER. You're gonna need a bigger boat!

 Dreyfuss and Shaw react disparagingly.

SHAW. Jesus…

SCHEIDER. …Sorry. I really love that line.

DREYFUSS. Did you make that line up?

SCHEIDER. No, Steven yelled it out just before he called action. But I nailed it!!

SHAW. Whoopty-do.

 Dreyfuss gets up.

DREYFUSS. You have nine children? You know, they sell prophylactics at any reputable drugstore.

SHAW. *(Sarcastic.)* Hahaha! How about you, Roy?

SCHEIDER. Just one—little girl. Do any of yours want to be actors?

SHAW. Christ, I hope not! It's a shrivelling profession, isn't it? Brutal for women.

SCHEIDER. There are worse jobs.

SHAW. You know what I mean. It's no job for a grown-up. Actors are children, aren't they? Present company excepted.

 Dreyfuss has got his hand caught putting on the sleeve of his coat, and Shaw gestures to Dreyfuss as if to negate his last sentence.

SCHEIDER. So what's a "grown-up" occupation? Should we all join the army?

DREYFUSS. Jesus, count me out—that shit's not for me. They didn't get me in 'Nam. I was a "conscientious objector." I worked in a hospital in LA.

SHAW. Haha!

DREYFUSS. What? Hey, it was plenty dangerous in that hospital!

SHAW. Yes, I'm certain you stubbed your toe on more than one occasion!

DREYFUSS. Hey screw you, man! What, I have to apologise because I didn't put on a uniform and go about killing people?

SCHEIDER. Nobody says you have to apologise for anything, Richard.

DREYFUSS. Yeah, well I got morals, principles. "Give peace a chance!" That's what I say. Nonviolence—talk things over. Hell, if Nixon and Kissinger and Brezhnev and Minh and Mao all got together and smoked a little weed all our problems would be solved!

SHAW. How profound.

    Beat.

You sound like a village idiot!

SCHEIDER. *(To Dreyfuss.)* Richard, I take your point, and god knows 'Nam is 'Nam, but don't you think sometimes you have to fight—maybe even die—for what you believe in?

    During this last exchange, Dreyfuss has begun to feel seasick.

DREYFUSS. I think I'm gonna throw up.

    Dreyfuss dashes off onto the deck and leans over the side as if to throw up.

SCHEIDER. Well that was something of an overreaction.

SHAW. Hasn't got his sea legs yet!

SCHEIDER. You know he adores you.

SHAW. He adores himself.

SCHEIDER. No, he does, he's very keen for you to introduce him to Harold Pinter.

SHAW. *(Laughs.)* Good god! What a car crash that would be.

SCHEIDER. Yes, I'd heard he was quite a character.

SHAW. He'd eat Richard alive. All that would be left would be a pile of bones.

    Dreyfuss returns to the cabin gingerly.

DREYFUSS. I'm okay. False alarm!

    Scheider takes out a handkerchief and blows his nose loudly.

SCHEIDER. Jesus! It's been two weeks and I still can't get the stink of that rotting fish out of my nose.

DREYFUSS. That shark was ripe when it came out of the box and it only got worse.

SCHEIDER. It makes sense, so—I looked this up, it's fascinating—sharks are one of the quickest species to decompose. It's because they're so primitive—they're, like, four hundred million years old. They're older than trees! No skeletons, just cartilage.

DREYFUSS. Sharks don't have skeletons? Nobody told me this.

SCHEIDER. And get this: Sharks have survived five mass-extinction events.

DREYFUSS. Five?

SCHEIDER. Yeah, and scientists figure there's going to be another one. Probably gonna be something to do with the weather—everything'll get real hot, humans'll die, mammals, but the sharks are just gonna keep on swimming. Hell, they might end up being the dominant species.

SHAW. So, if this film survives, perhaps it'll be watched by sharks one day.

DREYFUSS. Yeah—but to them it'll be a tragedy about a mild-mannered shark just going about his day eating a few people who gets senselessly murdered by three assholes!

> *They laugh.*

SHAW. That's very funny…two sharks leaving the cinema, and one says to the other "Well I quite liked it, apart from the ending."

SCHEIDER. I suppose that puts it all into perspective. The human race won't exist some day and here we are worrying about a stupid movie.

DREYFUSS. Hey, don't knock this "stupid movie," man. This is gonna make us famous.

SHAW. Is *that* why you're doing this?

DREYFUSS. Well who doesn't want to be a movie star?

SHAW. Speak for yourself! I'd rather be known for my writing. Jesus! The problem with the acting profession these days is that every little pissant wants to be a movie star, but nobody wants to play a Wednesday matinee at the…Stockton-on-Tees Forum! I had this bellboy come up to me the other day who told me he'd love to be famous like me. He'd got it the wrong way round. Fame is the by-product. It is the shit of art!

DREYFUSS. Okay, man, okay, calm down! Christ! I'm an artist, okay, I want to make art. If I happen to make a million bucks, get blown a hell of a lot, maybe make the cover of *Time* magazine along the way, then where's the harm? You think Shakespeare didn't get blown? Sure he did!

SHAW. So put your money where your mouth is, for god's sake! There are plenty of theatres in this country!

DREYFUSS. Well that's what I'd love to do… You know Harold Pinter, right?

Shaw and Scheider exchange a glance.

SHAW. Mr. Pinter and I have worked together on a number of occasions, yes.

DREYFUSS. What's he like?

SHAW. He is a great man. He is also an accomplished sprinter. He used to sprint for his county.

SCHEIDER. Pinter the sprinter.

SHAW. *(Sarcastic.)* Well done, Roy!

DREYFUSS. Well…do you think you could, you know, put in a good word for me? I'd love to do, you know, serious theatre work in some of his stuff—on Broadway, or London even. Do you think you could do that?

SHAW. Alright! If you're deadly serious, I'll give you his number. Don't fuck it up. Pinter is a very friendly man, Richard.

Shaw writes down Pinter's number and gives it to Dreyfuss.

SCHEIDER. Huh.

SHAW. There's nothing he enjoys more than chatting to people who appreciate his work. Just call him up—he's an early riser by the way—and say "Harold"—make sure you use his first name, he can't bear formality—"Harold, let's work together!"

SFX: Launch approaches.

DREYFUSS. Yeah?

SHAW. Yes! The other thing he likes is when people come up with theories as to what his plays are about. He gets a tremendous kick out of that.

DREYFUSS. Ooh, that's great because I've got one of those—the, what's it called, oh yeah, *The Dumb Waiter*, they're dead, right? And they're in hell.

SHAW. In hell? Oh that's very good. He won't have heard that one before.

DREYFUSS. That's great, cos I…

> *SFX: Launch strikes boat.*

Just a moment.

> *Exit Dreyfuss.*

SCHEIDER. Robert?

SHAW. Hmm?

SCHEIDER. Do you ever think you're too hard on him?

SHAW. It is the grit in the oyster that produces the pearl, Roy. I am that grit. He's giving a better performance because of me.

SCHEIDER. So…that's why you're doing this—making his life hell—to improve his performance?

SHAW. Of course.

> *Beat.*

What?

SCHEIDER. Nothing—it's just um…I'm not sure that's what it is.

> *Reenter Dreyfuss.*

DREYFUSS. You're not going to believe this… They get the replacement shark, they strap it to the rig, they take it underwater, they bring it back up and it's got a huge dent in its chin. Fucking thing looks like Kirk Douglas.

SCHEIDER. So?

DREYFUSS. So they got to take it back to base and hammer the goddamn dent out of it.

SCHEIDER. Ah shit.

DREYFUSS. Jim says we might as well call it a day. Fog's moved in anyway. Sorry guys.

SCHEIDER. Jesus!

DREYFUSS. I know. What a waste of time.

SHAW. FUCKING CHRIST!

SCHEIDER. Easy, Robert.

SHAW. My fucking visa's running out, for Christ's sake! I've got what—two or three days left, and then they tax the shit out of me! I'll owe the fucking IRS for the fucking *Sting* and *Pelham 123*! I already spend every spare day in Canada or bloody Bermuda!

SCHEIDER. Hey, come on, we'll go back to the hotel bar, have ourselves a steak, have a drink. Maybe even some clam chowder, huh?

DREYFUSS. Huh, great!

Dreyfuss and Scheider leave.

SHAW. Be with you in a moment!

Shaw looks at the script, throws it down in frustration, has a swig, then looks around for somewhere to hide the bottle, puts it under a tarpaulin, then exits.

SFX: Sound of launch leaving.

Scene 2

They are playing a card game, Oh Hell. Shaw deals seven cards to each of them as they converse.

SHAW. *(To Dreyfuss.)* That was quite a performance you gave earlier today, Richard, throwing up between takes.

DREYFUSS. Oh god…

Dreyfuss exits quickly and breathes sea air on deck.

SHAW. So what's in the paper today then, Roy?

SCHEIDER. Aside from Nixon? War. Disease. Famine. Bombs. Terrorists. Riots. Religious maniacs. You know, the usual.

SHAW. *(Sings.)* What a wonderful world…

Dreyfuss leans over the back and throws up.

Thar she blows. So what are your plans today Roy, in the extremely likely event that they don't get that bloody shark operational?

SCHEIDER. Oh you know, go through my lines for the scar scene, not that there are that many. If it warms up I'll go out on deck and catch a few rays.

SHAW. Again? Good god. You were out there all day yesterday, man. It's pathological!

SCHEIDER. You should try it!

SHAW. I can think of better things to do than gaze at my navel.

SCHEIDER. I think there's a spiritual element to it. Sitting there, soaking in the heat, listening to the ocean, the birds, letting your mind breathe; it's almost like meditating.

>*Dreyfuss reenters.*

SHAW. You're beginning to sound like our resident beatnik.

SCHEIDER. Sunshine is healthy.

DREYFUSS. You know, I wasn't going to say anything, Roy, but has it occurred to you that you're much browner than you were at the beginning of the shoot? What are you going to do if they need pick-ups?

SCHEIDER. Pfft! They can do anything in postproduction these days.

SHAW. Shame they can't fix my speech! Come on, let's bid. Three.

SCHEIDER. …Two.

DREYFUSS. I will also say two, you pussies.

SHAW. Can't say two.

DREYFUSS. Why not?

SHAW. It can't add up. I explained this!

SCHEIDER. Somebody has to suffer.

DREYFUSS. Why does somebody always have to suffer?

SHAW. It's the law of the universe!

DREYFUSS. Alright, fuck it, three.

>*They play. Dreyfuss wins the hand but doesn't follow suit. Then leads a club.*

SHAW. *(Looking at the previous hand.)* Hold on, hold on! In the first hand I played the ace of clubs, and you trumped it with the two of hearts. Now you just played a club.

DREYFUSS. So?

SHAW. You have to follow suit, you arsehole!

DREYFUSS. Shit, I forgot, I'm sorry.

> *Shaw throws his cards in Dreyfuss's face.*

SCHEIDER. I would have won that, you know…

SHAW. YES, YES!

SCHEIDER. I would have won…

> *Blackout.*

Scene 3—Indianapolis (Flashback)

> *SFX: Sound of film being rewound through editing suite.*
>
> *Lights up.*
>
> *Shaw, Dreyfuss, and Scheider in their Indianapolis positions, scripts at the table.*
>
> *The crew are in the cabin area, out of sight.*

FIRST ASSISTANT DIRECTOR.   *(Voice-over.)* Lighting!… Overhead!… Okay: Quiet please! Rehearsing… And…whenever you're ready, gentlemen…

SHAW. "That was the USS Indianapolis, Mr. Hooper. You've heard of that, right? Well, I was there. Let me tell you about the USS Indianapolis. It was 1945, chief. The Pacific was filled with Japanese submarines. They were everywhere. We'd just left the island of Tinian, a lovely place, chief."

Oh for god's sake, I can't say this! It's duller than my tax return.

> *He picks up the script and reads the rest out loud, quickly getting more and more exasperated.*

I mean, listen to this: "In the middle of the second day, some of us started to go crazy from the thirst. One fella cried out he saw a river, another claimed he saw a waterfall, some started to drink the ocean and choked on it, and some left our little group squares and swam off alone lookin' for islands and the sharks took them right away. It was mainly the young fellas that did that—the older ones stayed where they was."

For fuck's sake! It goes on for FIVE pages like this!

SPIELBERG. *(Voice-over.)* Alright, Robert, we'll give it back to John.

SHAW. No, no, no, don't give it back to Milius! *I'd* like to take a crack at it. There's some gold in there somewhere. Let me take it away and I'll write it myself.

SPIELBERG. *(Voice-over.)* Okay, Robert, take a shot at it.

SHAW. Thank you, Steven.

FIRST ASSISTANT DIRECTOR. *(Voice-over.)* Moving on, everybody!

> *Fade to black.*

Scene 4—Interlude 1

> *A scene lasting approximately one minute, designed to show the glacial pace of filmmaking. It signifies time, weather, waiting.*

> *Shaw is in the cabin, furiously scribbling and crossing out, rewriting the Indianapolis speech.*

Scene 5

> *Shaw is asleep. Scheider is reading the* New York Times. *Pause.*

> *SFX: Sound of launch approaching.*

SCHEIDER. Okay, here's another interesting fact—"Honey is the only food that does not spoil. Honey from the tombs of the Egyptian pharaohs has been tasted by archaeologists, and found to be edible."

> *Shaw snores.*

Am I boring you, Robert?

> *SFX: Boat bump.*

DREYFUSS. *(Unseen.)* WOO-HOO! OH, YES SIRREE, BOB!

SCHEIDER. Shhh! For crying out loud!

Enter Dreyfuss, holding Variety *excitedly.*

DREYFUSS. Oh my god! It's a hit! I'm in a hit! A fucking hit! *(Reads.)* "Kravitz, played by a continually grinning, scratching, nervous-making-yet-vulnerable Richard Dreyfuss, comes across effectively and with force."

SHAW. Would you kindly fuck off, boy?

DREYFUSS. And look in the *Times*! *(Pointing to Scheider's paper.)* There— *(Reads.)* "Not a bad performance in the film." Not a bad performance!

SHAW. Oh, Christ on a bicycle!

DREYFUSS. This is it! I'm big, I'm officially big. I'm going to be feted in Sardi's, and Elaine's. You ever eaten at Elaine's, Roy?

SCHEIDER. Nope.

DREYFUSS. Well dinner's on me the next time you're in town. The food stinks, but the clientele are the crème de la crème.

SHAW. Are you aware just how much you sound like a cheap prick?

DREYFUSS. Oh, you're just hung-over from drinking all night with Thornton Wilder.

Dreyfuss gets down on the floor and starts push-ups…

SHAW. It hurts me to hear you even say his name, boy. I wish you had a scintilla of his class.

SCHEIDER. Oh man, I wish I'd been there. What did you talk about?

SHAW. Writing. Life. Real things. Oh Christ…I need my stomach lining… Would you help me out, Roy…?

Scheider brings water and glass as if this has happened before. Thank you.

Shaw takes out a packet of Alka-Seltzer, adds it, and drinks.

DREYFUSS. *(Referring to push-ups.)* Six.

SHAW. What's happening on set?

DREYFUSS. The usual.

SHAW. Still…trying to fix the shark?

DREYFUSS. Yup.

SHAW. Right, let's have a game. Poker?

SCHEIDER. Crap, I left the cards in my street clothes.

SHAW. Alright…shove ha'penny?

DREYFUSS. Excuse me?

SHAW. Shove ha'penny. It's a pub game. Let me show you. Out of the way, boy. (*Demonstrating.*) You take a coin, put it on the table, hit it with your finger, try to get it as far as you can without touching the sides or the edge. Whoever goes furthest is the winner.

DREYFUSS. And this is a real game?

SHAW. This is a real game. Best of five. One-hundred-dollar entry.

DREYFUSS. A HUNDRED DOLLARS?!

SHAW. Come on! Roy?

DREYFUSS. Oh, I see, this is a shakedown!

SCHEIDER. Come on, Richard, what else are we gonna do?

DREYFUSS. I don't know. Work on my part?

SHAW. Won't do any good.

DREYFUSS. Very amusing. Call me crazy but I take this movie seriously.

SHAW. This is not a movie, this is—a trifle, an entertainment.

DREYFUSS. You know, art and entertainment are not mutually exclusive.

SCHEIDER. He's got a point there. I mean, take…*Casablanca*— you like *Casablanca*, right, Robert?

SHAW. "Kiss me, kiss me as if it were the last time…" Of course I like *Casablanca*, Roy—one of Bogie's finest.

SCHEIDER. Well, did they know they were making a "great movie," or were they just making a trifle?

SHAW. I get what you're saying lads, but I still think this film is destined for the dustbin of history—like the other big beasts of this decade: *The Towering Inferno*, *The Exorcist*, *Love Story*, *Airport*. Do you think anyone's going to remember any of those?

DREYFUSS. I kinda liked *Love Story*.

SHAW. That's because you're young. …And an idiot. You barely know how to wipe your own arse.

DREYFUSS. I resent that! I've been wiping my ass perfectly adequately since I was twenty!

SHAW. Look, are we going to stand around all day bickering like schoolgirls or are we going to play shove ha'penny?

DREYFUSS. I vote for bickering like schoolgirls!

SHAW. Come on, you degenerates!

> *Shaw preps the game.*

I don't have any ha'pennies so quarters'll have to do.

DREYFUSS. What the fuck is a "ha'penny"?

SHAW. Half a penny! It's perfectly simple—

SCHEIDER. Two ha'pennies to a penny, twelve pennies to a shilling, two shillings to a florin, ten florins to a pound.

SHAW. On the nose! And a guinea?

SCHEIDER. Twenty-one shillings!

SHAW. I'll drink to that!

> *Shaw retrieves a half bottle of blended scotch whisky from a cranny in the cabin. This should be timed to finish by the time he reaches for the bottle strapped to the underside of the table.*

DREYFUSS. You're making this up!

SHAW. Of course we're not. Right—a hundred dollars in the pot.

> *Shaw plonks his hat on the table to act as a pot, and puts in a hundred.*

Come on!

DREYFUSS. WHAT?

SCHEIDER. Here you go.

> *Scheider puts some notes in the hat.*

SHAW. *(To Dreyfuss.)* Right, now you—Cough up, boy!

DREYFUSS. Why don't you shove that ha'penny up your ass?!

SHAW. The money!

DREYFUSS. I don't have a hundred on me!

SCHEIDER. You were certainly flashing your cash around when you were flirting with that waitress last night!

DREYFUSS. Fine!

> *Dreyfuss reluctantly hands over various dollar bills.*

Okay, let's play your stupid fucking limey game.

> *Shaw places the hat on the table.*

SHAW. Observe, gentlemen.

> *Shaw puts a coin on the table, hits it, and it's a good one.*

Not bad. You next, Roy.

SCHEIDER. Why do I get the impression that this was how you misspent your youth, Robert?

> *Scheider has a go, not quite as good.*

SHAW. Pretty good, Roy. Pretty good for a first try.

SCHEIDER. Why thank you.

SHAW. *(To Dreyfuss.)* Now you, boy.

DREYFUSS. Okay.

> *Dreyfuss limbers up, cracks knuckles. He places his coin on the table… Shaw invades his space.*

Hey! Can you back off a little?

SHAW. *(Sarcastic.)* Terribly sorry!

> *Shaw moves back. Dreyfuss fails with his shot.*

Hahaha! Oh, bad luck!

DREYFUSS. Goddamn it!

SHAW. Nerves get the better of you?

DREYFUSS. The fucking coin was bent!

SHAW. Oh dear me boy, it's a bad workman who blames his tools. That's one to me. Round two.

> *Shaw makes a reasonable shot.*

Yes! Ba ba boom!

> *Scheider makes a better shot.*

SCHEIDER. Would you look at that!

SHAW. No, no, Roy, you weren't behind the line.

SCHEIDER. What line?!

>*Shaw whips out a pencil and places it at the start line.*

SHAW. *This* line—forgot to mention it!

DREYFUSS. What the hell?!

SHAW. Come on! No cheating!

>*Scheider makes a bad shot.*

SCHEIDER. Ah, shit.

SHAW. Sorry, Roy.

SCHEIDER. How many of these games do you know?

SHAW. Oh quite a few—Jenkins, penny football, pitch-and-toss. We must play pitch-and-toss.

>*Dreyfuss makes a winning shot.*

DREYFUSS. YES!! Oh yeah!

SHAW. Alright. Alright—don't get too full of yourself, boy. That's one to you.

DREYFUSS. It sure is, buddy. Okay—here we go!

>*Dreyfuss plays a bad shot.*

Shit!

SHAW. Pride comes before a fall, eh laddie? Roy?

SCHEIDER. Perhaps this is my chance to redeem myself.

>*Scheider takes another bad shot.*

Perhaps not.

SHAW. *(Singing.)*
>Farewell and adieu to you fair Spanish ladies
>Farewell and adieu to you ladies of Spain!

>*Shaw closes his eyes and makes a good shot.*

Yes!

SCHEIDER. Remarkable.

DREYFUSS. *(To Shaw.)* You're a hustler. He's a fucking hustler!

SHAW. *(Flicks a V and then the middle finger at Dreyfuss.)* That's two to me, and one to you!

DREYFUSS. Okay, okay—get on with it.

SHAW. *(Singing.)*

For we've received orders for to sail back to Boston…

Shaw hits the side.

DREYFUSS. You hit the side!

SHAW. BUGGER!

SCHEIDER. Oh, that's not so good, Robert!

DREYFUSS. What were you saying about pride coming before a fall?

SHAW. The table surface is irregular!

DREYFUSS. Hey, now who's blaming his tools?

Scheider makes a terrible shot.

SCHEIDER. Just can't seem to get the hang of this game.

DREYFUSS. Okay gentlemen, step back. Make way for Deadeye Dreyfuss.

SHAW. Get on with it!

Dreyfuss makes a good shot.

DREYFUSS. Yes!

SCHEIDER. Oh well done Richard! Have you played this before?

DREYFUSS. Yeah, we play a lot of shove ha'penny in Beverly Hills.

SHAW. That's two–all to us.

DREYFUSS. I wonder what I'm going to buy with my three hundred bucks?

SHAW. I'm going to grind you into the dirt, boy.

SCHEIDER. Uh, you know, Robert, I don't know if anyone's ever told you this, but you're kinda competitive.

SHAW. You don't know the half of it!

He slams his hand down on Dreyfuss's coin as he's about to shoot.

When I was seven my father moved the whole family, lock, stock, and barrel, to the Orkneys—to the coast of Scotland. A bloody inhospitable place. I was the only boy in the entire school with an English accent. The other children made my life hell. I'm sure it would have been worse if I'd been able to understand a word they were saying…I was obsessed with football—

DREYFUSS. You mean soccer?

SHAW. No, *football*! The first thing I wanted to do in the Orkneys was to join the school team, but they turned me down, the bastards. Said I wasn't good enough. But it was because I was English, because of the accent. So *(Laughs.)* I formed my own team. I went round the whole school and I rounded up all the other misfits they'd turned down—the Irish lad, the fat boy, the boy with the inch-thick spectacles. I found ten of them, and I was the captain. I trained those boys every day out there on the icy playing fields and then we challenged the school team to a match—

DREYFUSS. *(Interrupting.)* And you beat them ten–zero!

SHAW. …Four–nil, actually. Have I told this story before?!

DREYFUSS. No, but we've all seen *The Magnificent Seven*.

SHAW. Are you doubting my word?!

DREYFUSS. Oh come on Robert, please—

SCHEIDER. *(Intervening.)* Now, Richard, no punching below the belt. Let's everybody calm down, four weeks is a long time to be stuck together.

SHAW. Four weeks is a long time to be stuck on a slow boat to China with Brigitte Bardot and Rachel Welch. With you two it's a fucking eternity!

SCHEIDER. Come on, let's play. I'll go first, as I'm bound to do badly.

> *Scheider makes another bad shot.*

SHAW. Come on boy. Two–all. It's do or die.

DREYFUSS. Alright. Hands don't fail me now.

SHAW. You'll never do it you little punk.

> *Dreyfuss makes a mediocre shot.*

DREYFUSS. FUCK!

> *Shaw picks up the hat of money and goads him.*

SHAW. *(Singing.)*
> I've been a wild rover for many a year
> And I've spent all my money on whisky and beer
> And now I'm returning with gold in great store
> And I never will play the wild rover no more

Dreyfuss and Scheider join in as if they have sung together before.

SHAW, DREYFUSS, and SCHEIDER. *(Singing.)*
And it's no, nay, never!

Shaw bangs the table in rhythm.

No, nay, never, no more
Will I play the wild rover
No never, no more!

Shaw overshoots and loses.

SHAW. OH SHIIIIIT!

DREYFUSS. OH MY GOD! OH MY GOD!

Dreyfuss runs outside. Scheider enjoys the moment.

SCHEIDER. I don't believe it!

DREYFUSS. *(Calling to the heavens.)* THANK YOU GOD! THANK YOU JEHOVAH!

Dreyfuss runs back in, takes the money hat, and overcelebrates, falling to the ground.

Come to poppa! Hoo boy!

SHAW. ALRIGHT, ALRIGHT, YOU WIN! …Goddamn it!

DREYFUSS. Boy, you are such a bad loser!

SHAW. Dumb luck, I guess!

Dreyfuss notices a bottle of whisky under the table.

DREYFUSS. Why is there a bottle strapped to the underside of the table?

Shaw leans forward to look at Dreyfuss fiercely. Pause.

SHAW. In case it's needed.

DREYFUSS. May I have a drink?

Beat. Shaw pours a cup.

SHAW. Knock yourself out.

DREYFUSS. You know, there's a question I've been wanting to ask you…

SHAW. And what might that be?

DREYFUSS. Why do you drink so much?

SHAW. To cope with smart-arses like you, Richard.

DREYFUSS. No. Seriously.

Shaw offers Scheider a dram.

SHAW. Roy?

SCHEIDER. Uh…just a finger.

Shaw pours a finger.

SHAW. I'm English. I have to drink—to cope with the climate. If the English didn't drink we'd have died out years ago.

DREYFUSS. Nah, I don't buy that. I've known plenty of Brits that don't hit the bottle. I want the real reason—what, is it the "artistic temperament" shtick?

SHAW. Why does anyone drink? Why do you smoke that stuff that makes you giggle? Why'd you snort that powder that makes your eyes water? I've seen you coming out of the boghouse red-eyed, sniffing like a dog. Now why would you do that?

DREYFUSS. I'm not gonna deny I like getting high occasionally.

SHAW. Yes. I suppose that's how it starts. My god, I loved to drink when I was young. It was such pleasure going to the pub and getting smashed after a show. People talk about there being a cultural pressure to drink in England, but as a young man it felt natural, wonderful, it freed us up. We talked about art, politics, we were theatrical revolutionaries, we were going to change the world!… Working with George Devine at the Royal Court, doing *The Long and The Short and The Tall* with Peter O'Toole… Heaven.

SCHEIDER. I think you did change the world. It's just that the world tends to revert to type.

SHAW. Bless you, Roy. Anyway…we were competitive. We'd pride ourselves on still being able to function after a tidal wave of booze! Still standing, like a bull peppered with banderillas. I don't know at what point drink became a part of me…perhaps even before I was born. My father was an alcoholic, you know. A *real* alcoholic, not just a barroom brawler, or a dilettante drinker like O'Toole; a proper, hollow-legged drunkard… Trouble is, these days I find that it interferes with my writing. I tried to quit last year…but I found myself with a drink in my hand as a reward for a week of not drinking.

Shaw empties the bottle.

Cheers!

They drink.

Well, we do appear to be having a real old heart-to-heart, don't we?

As Shaw says this he reaches for the hidden half bottle of blended scotch whisky under the table and pours. Beat.

How'd you get that beautiful broken nose, Mr. Scheider?

SCHEIDER. The 1946 Diamond Gloves Tournament. I was thirteen. I lost by technical knockout to Myron Greenberg.

DREYFUSS. You were a boxer?

SCHEIDER. Welterweight.

SHAW. Now that's a real man's profession. Not like this—poncing about on a soundstage covered in makeup like a prostitute!

DREYFUSS. Was your father a boxer?

SCHEIDER. He was an auto mechanic. He ran the local gas station; typical blue-collar guy but full of contradictions. He hates everyone: Blacks, Catholics, Jews, Communists. Yet he married a Catholic, was friendly with the Jewish people who ran the local store, and his dentist was Black. But behind closed doors, all that bile came pouring out. He made derogatory remarks right in front of us.

SHAW. Did you fight with him?

SCHEIDER. Yeah! He beat the hell out of me. My biggest crime was disagreeing with him. I realised as an adolescent that what my father was telling me wasn't true. I took the beatings to let him know he wasn't fooling me. My mother couldn't intervene. I got the support I needed from a man who worked at the gas station. One of my father's Black employees, as a matter of fact. A guy named Friend Avery.

DREYFUSS. I bet you wanted to run as far as you could from the family business.

SCHEIDER. It's complicated. I was a sick kid. I had rheumatic fever, I'd get these horrendous attacks. My mother stayed home to take care of me. She thought I was gonna die. I spent an awful lot of time in bed. Thinking, dreaming, creating. A lot of fantasy worlds that probably led me into acting. To this day I cannot stand to be in a room with an unmade bed…or drawn drapes. I want to throw them open and let in the fresh air, the sunshine…

DREYFUSS. Well, my dad wanted me to be a lawyer. I know—typical Jewish family, you gotta be a lawyer, or a doctor. You may find this difficult to believe but I was kind of an irritating kid…

SHAW. No, no!

DREYFUSS. Yeah, yeah…short, scrawny, overconfident… I saw *The Great White Hope* on Broadway. I didn't like the play, didn't like the direction, but in two scenes Jane Alexander and James Earl Jones got me so badly, so deeply, that I was not only crying, I was snotting gracelessly down my face! Beyond hope! But when it ended, I leapt into the air—I was wearing my little bar mitzvah suit on a trip to the city—and I was shaken to my core. So later I was sitting with my mother at the kitchen table and I told her I want to be an actor and she said "*Well, don't just talk about it, do it!*" So I got up, and I auditioned for a play at the West Side Jewish Community Center.

> *Shaw tops up Dreyfuss.*

Dad was not happy. But you should hear him now on the subject of "My son, the famous actor."

SCHEIDER. Yeah, my dad's the same—when I was nominated for *French Connection*, he wouldn't even come to the phone, but now he gets a real kick out of it!

> *Beat.*

Your father still around, Robert?

SHAW. No… He killed himself when I was twelve.

SCHEIDER. Shit.

DREYFUSS. Really?

SHAW. Oh yes. Christ, he's been gone such a long time. He was a Victorian… Funny to think that, isn't it? Different era. An extraordinary man…marvellous man. He was a doctor in the Orkneys, those terrible islands where there's wind and sea and you get hundred-mile-an-hour gales. He was the lighthouse doctor, and he used to keep a medical bag on each island, and when the boat couldn't get in because the sea was so rough, he used to tie a rope around his waist, and jump into the freezing water and swim ashore, and there would be his medical bag, and he would deliver whatever baby was to be delivered.

SCHEIDER. Wow.

SHAW. I don't know whether being in the First World War drove him to drink… He used to sit on the end of my bed and cry when he thought I was asleep. I've always wished he could have lived a little longer, because I felt I could have helped him. Which all boys feel, I think if their father dies, whether it's in a war—it's Vietnam, it's drugs, it's drink, or whatever the hell it is, you always feel, if you're a proud son, that you could have…*said something.* —For years, I dreamt my father was walking with me in a beautiful place and I was holding his hand and I'd say: "Everything'll be alright, Dad."

> *Beat.*

Well, I never got to that… —He wanted me to be a doctor. It was a school teacher that got me into the theatre, a man named Wilkes. He took us up to the West End. I saw Gielgud's *Hamlet*. Dad was gone by then.

> *Shaw drinks again.*

It's funny. I always thought I must live at least as long as he did. I don't know why. Perhaps it's something all men feel.

SCHEIDER. How old was he when he died?

SHAW. Fifty-two.

SCHEIDER. And how old are you now?

SHAW. Forty-seven. Five more years to go…if I make it.

DREYFUSS. Yeah? Well… I can help with that.

> *Dreyfuss rises and grabs the bottle of whisky.*

SCHEIDER. Richard?

SHAW. What are you doing, boy?

DREYFUSS. I'm saving your life, pal!

> *Dreyfuss exits to stern.*

SCHEIDER. Uh Richard…

> *Dreyfuss holds the bottle over the side of the boat.*

SHAW. WHAT ARE YOU FUCKING DOING?!!!!

DREYFUSS. I shoulda done this weeks ago.

> *Dreyfuss drops bottle over side.*

SHAW. NOOOO!!

> *Dreyfuss reenters. Shaw grabs him by lapels.*

WHAT HAVE YOU DONE YOU FUCKING SWINE???

> *Shaw swings him round.*

I'LL KILL YOU! I'LL FUCKING KILL YOU!

> *Shaw grabs Dreyfuss by the throat.*

SCHEIDER. ROBERT!

SHAW. FUCKING LITTLE BASTARD!

DREYFUSS. *(Choking.)* You're choking me!

SCHEIDER. *(Trying to intervene like a boxing referee.)* THAT'S ENOUGH!

SHAW. NEVER TOUCH ANOTHER MAN'S BOOZE! DID NO ONE EVER TELL YOU THAT? NEVER TOUCH ANOTHER MAN'S BOOZE!

SCHEIDER. Let go of him, Robert, you're going to hurt him!

SHAW. I'M GONNA *KILL* HIM!

SCHEIDER. Robert! We are shooting a movie for Universal Pictures. If you kill him, they will sue you. They will sue your wife. Sue your kids. Hell, they may even sue me!

> *Beat. Shaw lets Dreyfuss go.*

DREYFUSS. Lunatic. You're a fucking lunatic! You could have injured me badly!

SHAW. Oh shut up you little cry baby! I barely touched you!

DREYFUSS. My whole life flashed in front of my eyes.

SCHEIDER. *(To Dreyfuss.)* It would seem your theatrical gesture backfired.

DREYFUSS. Yeah, I gotta say that played out a lot better in my head.

SHAW. *(To Dreyfuss.)* You owe me ten dollars for the bottle!

DREYFUSS. It was half-empty!

SHAW. GIMME THE MONEY!

DREYFUSS. FINE!

> *Dreyfuss throws a crumpled bill on the floor which Shaw retrieves.*

SHAW. Now I'll have to find someone to send down the liquor store.

DREYFUSS. Ah come on—don't tell me you don't have another bottle stashed around here somewhere.

SHAW. Maybe I have and maybe I haven't. You will never know.

DREYFUSS. Go fuck yourself! And another thing—that play of yours—*The Man in the Glass Booth*, that's anti-Semitic, man!

SHAW. I thought you called yourself an intellectual, boy! You've the mentality of a tabloid hack!

DREYFUSS. And I don't like you calling me "boy."

SHAW. Is that right, BOY?!!

SCHEIDER. Jesus you two! Please can you fucking relax? You're gonna give me a nervous breakdown!

> *Beat.*

We have got to finish this movie and get the hell outta here!

DREYFUSS. Yeah…yeah…I guess.

SCHEIDER. Now, come on. Please shake hands.

SHAW. What?!

SCHEIDER. C'mon.

> *Dreyfuss reluctantly offers his hand.*

DREYFUSS. I'm sorry I threw your liquor overboard, Robert.

> *Beat.*

SHAW. Very well Richard, I accept your apology.

> *Shaw and Dreyfuss shake—then Shaw crushes Dreyfuss's hand.*

> *SFX: A launch approaches.*

But if you ever lay a hand on one of my bottles again I will put you in the ground!

> *Shaw releases him, Dreyfuss rubs his hand.*

DREYFUSS. You know what I like about you Robert? You're so easygoing, so carefree… Just remind me not to get you angry again.

SHAW. Oh that wasn't me getting angry, Richard. When I'm angry you'll know about it.

SFX: The launch hits the boat.

SFX: Radio static.

Dreyfuss exits. Shaw and Scheider sit.

SCHEIDER. Thank you for not putting him in the ground.

SHAW. My dear fellow, I am a professional.

Dreyfuss reenters.

DREYFUSS. Sounds incredible, but the weather's right, there are no boats in shot, and Bruce is actually working. Roy, they're ready for us!

SCHEIDER. Really?

DREYFUSS. Yeah, quick, come on before any of those three things change.

SCHEIDER. Okay okay.

Scheider exits.

SHAW. Oh Richard—a piece of advice before they start shooting…

DREYFUSS. Yeah?

SHAW. Mind your mannerisms!

Exit Dreyfuss.

Fade to black.

Scene 6—Indianapolis 2 (Flashback)

SFX: Sound of film being rewound through editing suite.

They're ready for the Indianapolis recording.

SPIELBERG. *(Voice-over.)* Okay, when you're ready Robert.

SHAW. Just a moment.

Shaw drinks from a half bottle of Irish whiskey.

Alright.

ASSISTANT DIRECTOR. *(Voice-over.)* Okay… Quiet on set everybody… Quiet please.

SHAW. "Japanese submarine slammed two torpedoes into her side, shief…"

ASSISTANT DIRECTOR. *(Voice-over.)* Sorry, Robert—we're not rolling.

SHAW. Oh, shit. My mistake!

Shaw drinks again.

ASSISTANT DIRECTOR. *(Voice-over.)* Okay, quiet on set! Camera?

CAMERA OPERATOR. *(Voice-over.)* Rolling.

ASSISTANT DIRECTOR. *(Voice-over.)* Sound?

SOUND RECORDIST. *(Voice-over.)* Speed.

ASSISTANT DIRECTOR. *(Voice-over.)* Mark it.

FOCUS PULLER. *(Voice-over.)*Scene 191, D. Take one.

SFX: Clack.

SPIELBERG. *(Voice-over.)* And action!

SHAW. "Japanese submarine slammed two torpedoes into her side, shief… We was comin' back from the island of Leyte… *(Laughs drunkenly.)* Christ…sorry…keep rolling! Japanese submarine slammed two torpedoes into our side, shief… We was comin' back from the island of Tinian to Leyte. We'd just delivered the bomb. The Hiroshima bomb. Eleven hundred men went into the water. Vessel went down in twelve minutes…"

Pause as he searches for the lines.

Oh Christ, what comes next…

CONTINUITY. *(Voice-over.)* Didn't see the first shark for about half an hour…

SHAW. What…?! Speak up, for god's sake!

DREYFUSS. Didn't see the first shark for about half an hour…

SHAW. Shut up, boy! Are you playing Quint now?! I know the bloody lines, fool, I fuckin' wrote them. Look at your furry little face! You're like a Chihuahua! You know, there is one part you could play in Shakespeare, boy! The Fool! *(Laughs.)* —You play Fool…I'll play Lear. How about that?

"You think I'll weep…
No, I'll not weep, I have full cause of weeping, you motherfuckers!
But this heart
Shall break into a hundred thousand flaws,
Or ere I'll weep… O fool, I shall go mad!"
You play Fool to my Lear, and I'll play Falstaff to your Chihuahua!

Shaw collapses with drunkenness.

SPIELBERG. *(Voice-Over.)* I think… Robert, I think we should leave it there.

Shaw tries to get up.

SHAW. Oh Christ, sorry, Steven.

Scheider helps Shaw to his unsteady feet.

ASSISTANT DIRECTOR. *(Voice-over.)* Alright, everybody. That's a wrap.

SHAW. Oh Roy, Roy, Roy, Roy my boy, you're a good man, very loyal, you can play Kent—or Gloucester, if you don't mind your eyes being gouged out… .

Scheider lays Shaw down on the bench.

Sorry, everybody! Sorry…

Shaw passes out.

Fade to black.

Scene 7—Interlude 2

A minute of a growing squall with thunder and lightning.

Dreyfuss and Scheider are in the cabin.

Dreyfuss, anxious, with his back to the cabin wall.

Scheider, meditative and queasy, is at the table.

Both are rocking with the boat.

Shaw is outside in the storm, hanging onto the rail.

As the storm grows and lightning strikes, he lets go of the rail briefly and dares the storm to take him—like King Lear on the heath ("Blow winds and crack your cheeks!") playing with death.

Scene 8

Lights up.

Dreyfuss is at the table replaying lines. He's already shot. He gets more and more anxious, as he thinks he's messed up the scene.

DREYFUSS. "That's it. Goodbye. I'm not gonna waste my time arguing with a man who's lining up to be a hot lunch…"

Pause.

"That's it. Goodbye…"

Pause.

"That's it. Goodbye…"

Pause.

"That's it. Goodbye. I'm not gonna waste my time arguing with a man who's lining up to be a hot lunch…oh shit!"

He bows his head, beaten.

Dreyfuss's hands fall on Quint's cap. He puts it on.

(*With sinister frustration.*) Piece of advice, boy. Listen to me—when I was on the London stage playing *Macbeth* back in 1906, Sir Robertson Fuckwad said to me, he said to me "Shaw, you are the biggest douchebag I have ever had the misfortune to have met." And since that day, boy, I have striven, with the sweat of my brow and the strain of my sinew to become the largest douchebag in the history of the universe. And I have done it, boy, I have done it!

Now where's my booze? I've only had six bottles of rum today! I need more!

SFX: A launch approaches.

Dreyfuss does not notice Scheider appear and come to the door.

Dreyfuss finds a bottle.

Ah! Marvelous! Don't you think so, Roy?

SFX: A launch strikes the boat.

Dreyfuss takes off the cap and moves to Scheider's normal position.

(*Impersonating Scheider.*) Actually Robert, here's an interesting fact, interestingly enough.

Scheider enters and observes.

The douchebag is a contraceptive device first used by Martha Washington in the eighteenth century. Now isn't that interesting? Don't you think that's interesting?

SCHEIDER. Am I interrupting?

DREYFUSS. (*Rumbled.*) No, no, no! Just doing some lines. Script lines.

SCHEIDER. You want me to go over them with you?

DREYFUSS. There's no need… We already shot the scene.

SCHEIDER. Uh-huh… Why are you doing them, then?

DREYFUSS. Oh, just the usual… You know, torturing myself.

Scheider sits down and yawns.

Tired?

SCHEIDER. I didn't sleep last night.

DREYFUSS. (*Pruriently.*) Oh, ho, ho!

SCHEIDER. No…I was uh, watching TV. They had on a documentary of the war, and they were showing pictures of the burning monk, and the naked girl with the napalm burns and…I couldn't get the images out of my mind.

Pause.

DREYFUSS. Roy?

SCHEIDER. Yes?

DREYFUSS. Remind me to never double-date with you.

Scheider smiles.

Have they fixed the shark, perchance?

SCHEIDER. No, but that's not the current problem.

DREYFUSS. What is the "current" problem?

SCHEIDER. The townsfolk. The, uh, "local authorities." They're complaining about the set that Joe Alves built, you know—Quint's shack.

DREYFUSS. What?

Scheider goes to fetch a soft drink.

SCHEIDER. Well, it's thirty-eight feet high, but there's a twenty-four-foot limit in the local building code. So they want it demolished, rebuilt, proper concrete foundations, electrical connections, waste pipes, piles below sea level, and a permit, which takes six months to come through.

DREYFUSS. *(Growing frustration.)* But it's a fucking set! It's gonna be demolished in six days.

SCHEIDER. I know.

> *Scheider sits at the table to read the* New York Times.

DREYFUSS. Assholes.

SCHEIDER. I know.

DREYFUSS. God—those bastards deserve all the bad luck that comes their way. I curse every single one of them. May their limbs wither and their eyeballs burst in their skulls—as my father used to say.

SCHEIDER. Jesus. He sounds a real peach.

DREYFUSS. He walked out on the family on the night of my twenty-first birthday.

> *Pause.*

SCHEIDER. Sorry to hear that.

> *Beat.*

DREYFUSS. It's not exactly as if we ever played catch together.

> *Pause. Dreyfuss fidgets nervously. He wants to talk.*

Roy?

SCHEIDER. What?

DREYFUSS. Am I any good? As an actor?

SCHEIDER. What, are you fishing for compliments? Of course I think you're good, Richard!

DREYFUSS. Well I don't. I think maybe Robert's right, I'm a fake. I'm a phoney. I was on set yesterday and I didn't even know who I was. I didn't feel like Hooper and I didn't feel like me. I felt completely…disembodied.

SCHEIDER. Everyone feels like that sometimes.

DREYFUSS. They do? Do you ever feel like that?

SCHEIDER. Sure I do.

DREYFUSS. Yeah? Well everyone was looking at me yesterday like they knew! Like they knew I was a fake. Steven, Gottleib, Lorraine, James, Michael, everyone. Have they said anything to you about me?

SCHEIDER. What are you talking about?

DREYFUSS. Has Steven said anything about me? Or Gottleib?

SCHEIDER. Gottleib hasn't said anything about you.

DREYFUSS. So Steven *has* said something about me?

SCHEIDER. Neither of them has said anything! Richard, I hesitate to say this, but don't you think you're being a little paranoid?

DREYFUSS. Paranoid?! Is that what they're saying about me—I'm paranoid?! Oh shit—oh shit—

> *Dreyfuss starts to hyperventilate, holding his chest.*

SCHEIDER. Richard? Richard? Are you okay?

DREYFUSS. I'm…fine…huh…just…gimme…huh…a…minute.

SCHEIDER. Richard…you're hyperventilating… That means you're exhaling more than you're inhaling. You're breathing out carbon dioxide quicker than you're breathing in oxygen.

DREYFUSS. *(Struggling to breathe.)* Thanks…for…that…tidbit… Roy…very…interesting.

> *Dreyfuss gets up to go outside for air but collapses to his knees. Still gasping for breath. Scheider gets up to help.*

SCHEIDER. Jesus Richard, how much snow have you had this morning?

DREYFUSS. I haven't had any yet today!

SCHEIDER. Okay that's good, but you gotta stop doing that to yourself Richard! It's not healthy. It's irresponsible—we're shooting a movie here—there's a lot of people that are counting on you!

DREYFUSS. Oh!

> *Dreyfuss gets worse.*

SCHEIDER. Look, you've got to calm down.

> *Scheider searches for a solution. Takes his Zippo cigarette lighter from his pocket.*

Concentrate on the flame.

He flicks it on in front of Dreyfuss's face.

DREYFUSS. *(Recoiling from the flame.)* Gaaaagh!

SCHEIDER. SORRY... Sorry!

Scheider pulls it back.

SFX: A launch approaches.

Shaw climbs onto the boat.

Richard, it's right here. I want you to concentrate on the flame.

DREYFUSS. Which part?

SCHEIDER. What?

DREYFUSS. *(Still struggling to breathe.)* The blue part or the yellow part? WHICH PART?

SCHEIDER. All of it, Richard! Just breathe in, breathe out. Concentrate on the entire flame.

DREYFUSS. All I can see is the burning monk you were talking about!

Dreyfuss gets worse.

SCHEIDER. *(Putting his hand on Dreyfuss's shoulder.)* Richard, stop! Everything is okay. You're a wonderful actor.

SFX: A launch strikes the boat.

Dreyfuss falls into Scheider's arms and sobs. Scheider cradles him.

You're exactly where you're meant to be, Richard. You're wonderful. You're wonderful.

Shaw enters. It looks like they are in a romantic embrace.

SHAW. What the holy fuck are you two doing?

SCHEIDER. Take it easy Robert, Richard's having a panic attack.

SHAW. Oh, I see. I thought I'd stumbled into Woodstock for a moment!

SCHEIDER. I really think he needs some space, Robert.

SHAW. Oh for god's sake! What's the matter with you, Petunia?!

Dreyfuss explodes in Shaw's face.

DREYFUSS. JUST FUCK OFF ROBERT WOULD YOU?! FUUUUCK OFFFFF!

> *Dreyfuss collapses sobbing under the table. Scheider glances disbelieving at Shaw and then looks away. Pause. Shaw sits on the deck with the others. He considers the moment, then…*

SHAW. (*Slowly, gently, meaningfully—not Royal Shakespeare Company.*) "When, in disgrace with fortune and men's eyes,
I all alone beweep my outcast state,
And trouble deaf heaven with my bootless cries,
And look upon myself and curse my fate,
Wishing me like to one more rich in hope,
Featured like him, like him with friends possessed,
Desiring this man's art and that man's scope,
With what I most enjoy contented least;

> *Shaw takes out a half bottle of Jamaican rum.*

"Yet in these thoughts myself almost despising,
Haply I think on thee, and then my state,
(Like to the lark at break of day arising
From sullen earth) sings hymns at heaven's gate;
For thy sweet love remembered such wealth brings
That then I scorn to change my state with kings."

> *Shaw drinks. Dreyfuss looks up.*

> *Pause.*

I wrote that when I was five.

> *They all laugh.*

SCHEIDER. Where have you been?

SHAW. Highland Links. Shot eighty-eight.

DREYFUSS. Is that good or bad?

SHAW. I started out with two birdies on the front nine, but I fucked up coming back. Lost two balls. Putting was horrendous. Every time I'm about to hit my first shot, I say to myself "today's the day!" but it never is.

SCHEIDER. Why do you put yourself through it?

SHAW. I don't know? …It's the modern incarnation of an ancient fertility rite. It was invented by sex-starved Scottish shepherds. The ball is the sperm and the hole is the egg. You replicate the difficult and dangerous journey to conception, trying to get there first.

> *Shaw gets up to sit down on the bench. Scheider follows.*

SCHEIDER. Huh. I never thought about golf that way. Does this apply to other sports?

SHAW. Probably. In football the goal is the egg and the ball is the sperm, in basketball the hoop is the egg…

DREYFUSS. I don't think it works with baseball. There you have a guy trying to get his sperm past another guy, who is trying to hit his sperm out of the park.

SHAW. You're right… Baseball is a fruitless pursuit.

SCHEIDER. Well, whatever fertility rite you're performing it's certainly working.

DREYFUSS. I need some air.

> *Dreyfuss gets up to go out. Shaw hands him his spectacles as he leaves.*

SCHEIDER. You are full of surprises.

SHAW. Snifter?

SCHEIDER. No, thank you.

> *Shaw picks up the empty bottle of Irish whiskey Dreyfuss left on the table.*

SHAW. *(Wistfully.)* Now, if I mixed Jamaican rum and Irish whiskey together I wonder what it would make?

SCHEIDER. Trouble.

SHAW. God, he makes me feel so old.

SCHEIDER. You're hardly old, Robert.

SHAW. I know, but when I was his age I thought the world was my oyster, so full of possibility. But it was just an illusion. A mirage of unknown futures that all…disappear once you make a choice. The greatest thing about being young is the falsehood that the blank canvas will lead you to limitless adventure.

> *Pause.*

SCHEIDER. *(Grabbing a mug.)* Jeez. I think I will have that drink now.

SHAW. Man takes a drink,

> *Shaw pours Scheider a shot.*

Drink takes a drink,

> *Shaw pours himself a shot.*

Drink takes the man.

> *They clink their drinks.*

> *Lights fade.*

Scene 9

Lights up on Scheider reading his New York Times*.*

RADIO. *(Voice-over.)* Mr. Scheider, there are still boats in the shot. Go ahead and take your lunch.

> *Satisfied, Scheider sets down his newspaper. He disrobes down to his tight black Speedos. He folds his clothes carefully and places them on the seat, then he lights a cigarette and puts on his sunglasses. He picks up a deck chair and a beach bag containing his sun mirror and goes through the door onto the deck.*

> *Scheider unfolds a deck chair and lifts up his face to the sun. He then positions the chair so as to best face the sun and stretches before sitting down. He takes a deep breath in and out.*

SCHEIDER. Peace.

> *SFX: Boat air horn honks.*

> *Scheider waves then flips off the passing boat.*

> *He picks up his tanning mirror and unfolds it, resting it on his chest so as to reflect the sun's rays onto his face.*

RADIO. *(Voice-over.)* Mr. Scheider?

> *Scheider ignores the radio, quickly settles back into sunbathing.*

Pause.

Mr. Scheider, Mr. Scheider?

Pause.

Mr. Scheider?

Pause.

Mr. Scheider, please respond.

Pause.

Mr. Scheider, do you copy?

Suddenly Scheider turns his head and shouts at the radio.

SCHEIDER. SHUT UP!!

Pause.

Scheider returns to his sunbathing.

Long pause.

Thank you.

RADIO. *(Voice-over.)* Mr. Scheider, the sailboat's out of shot and the background is clear. Lunch is cancelled. We've got to shoot. Sending a boat over, please respond.

Scheider leaps up and picks up Quint's sawn-off baseball bat (priest) and lifts it over the radio, ready to smash it to pieces.

Mr. Scheider, can you pick up, please? Do you copy? Mr. Scheider? Mr. Scheider, can you come in? We are sending a boat, please be ready, we've got to shoot!

Scheider takes a very deep breath and manages to put the bat down. He smooths his hair. Deep breath.

Mr. Scheider, are you receiving?

SCHEIDER. *(Forcing himself to sound bright.)* I'll be right there!

Blackout.

Scene 10

Lights up revealing Shaw searching for alcohol under the hatch. On the floor…

DREYFUSS. Ahem!

SHAW. Oh, Christ, it's you!

DREYFUSS. What the hell are you doing?

SHAW. Last month I hid a bottle of Lagavulin in here so cunningly, with such Machiavellian guile, that I have subsequently been completely unable to find it.

DREYFUSS. You need it? I mean it's the last day, for Christ's sake.

SHAW. Yes, I need it.

DREYFUSS. Well, how hard can it be? Like Roy said, it's not that big a boat.

SHAW. That is a misquotation, my friend. Christ, I've been over every square inch of this place.

DREYFUSS. Well, I can help!

They both start to search the benches.

SHAW. If you think I'm letting you near any of my booze after that stunt you pulled!

DREYFUSS. I don't have a death wish. Jeez—But, come on, I'm really good at finding stuff. One time, we were in Italy…

SHAW. What were you doing in Italy?

DREYFUSS. Oh, we travelled a lot around Europe when I was a kid.

SHAW. You go to Ireland?

DREYFUSS. Ireland? Nope.

SHAW. Pity. It's a wonderful country. Of course the people are completely mad, but that's what's so wonderful about them. Do you know I once ordered spaghetti in a Cork restaurant and when it arrived it was still in the shape of the can?

DREYFUSS. They eat canned spaghetti?

SHAW. They eat pig's trotters and skirts and kidneys.

DREYFUSS. Jesus!

Dreyfuss keeps searching. Shaw goes into the fore cabin and comes out with a screwdriver.

SHAW. I live in County Mayo right by the shore of Lough Mask. The water's clear enough to drink. I can row across the lake to Paddy Walsh's pub, and have my choice of either Guinness or Smithwick's. That is if Paddy isn't out fishing for brown trout. No, I love the Irish—they're god's own people.

Shaw goes down on his knees to prise open another hatch.

Dreyfuss takes the screwdriver from Shaw to prevent him from causing damage.

DREYFUSS. Are you sure this bottle is in here?

SHAW. …No!

Dreyfuss goes on deck.

Oh, Christ! Now you've got me questioning myself. Did I drink the Lagavulin? You know they could do a marvellous game show on television—get in six drinkers, get them each to hide a bottle of scotch, then drink a bottle of scotch, and then they have to find the first one!

DREYFUSS. *(From outside.)* Yeah that sounds great. Real family fun.

Dreyfuss finds a bottle hidden under a railing. Enters triumphantly.

BINGO!

SHAW. Saints be praised! You're like a *truffle pig*, boy!!

Shaw gets two mugs.

Come on.

Shaw pushes him out on deck.

DREYFUSS. Uh, no, I better not, I—

SHAW. You wouldn't be refusing to drink with me, would you, Richard?

DREYFUSS. Okay, okay! Christ Robert. Fine!

Dreyfuss drinks with Shaw.

(Spluttering the strong scotch.) That's a twelve-year-old scotch— How'd you get it out here?

SHAW. Oh, I know someone who could get hold of moonshine in Saudi Arabia.

DREYFUSS. Who?

SHAW. Ned Lynch.

DREYFUSS. He sounds like a pirate.

SHAW. He probably comes from a long line of smugglers. He keeps me out of trouble, too. I've fired him several times but he's never accepted it.

DREYFUSS. You know, when we first started filming this fucking movie—several thousand years ago—I looked at you, and I thought, I'm going to figure out exactly where you end and Quint begins?

SHAW. Still not sure, eh?

DREYFUSS. And that's the way you like it!

SHAW. Where's Roy, by the way?

DREYFUSS. Oh, he's in the can. I think he's regretting the lobster bisque last night.

SHAW. That shellfish will get you in the end. Quite literally.

> *They drink…*

> *SFX: Loud sounds off—shark repair.*

Good god, it's the last day and they're still hammering on that bloody thing.

DREYFUSS. Do you ever feel stupid?

SHAW. Do I ever feel stupid?

DREYFUSS. Doing this job, I mean, here we are, the shark is broken—again—it's fucked, and Steven is asking for all these reaction shots to a thing that doesn't even exist! It just feels so goddamn stupid! Like when you're a little kid and you run around the neighbourhood like Superman

> *He demonstrates Superman.*

I don't know…it just feels so childish.

SHAW. At times, I've found myself utterly depressed with how ridiculous it all is, how seriously we all take ourselves; fame, adulation, money, agents, lawyers, producers, merchandising, it's all a crock of bullshit…

DREYFUSS. So you *do* feel stupid?

SHAW. Of course I bloody do! All actors do… You know, almost more than anything else I wish I'd been good enough to be a first-class rugby player. No matter what you do in the arts people can say they don't like it. They can say "Tolstoy is a second-rate novelist!" But when you score a try they can't take it away from you.

DREYFUSS. Do you think being an actor undermines your… masculinity?

SHAW. Oh fucking hell! Look, I'm not…a therapist, Richard. Have another drink.

DREYFUSS. Richard Benjamin just said that acting was not a fit profession for a mature man! Hoffman calls it womanish. Like there's something shameful about it—

SFX: Launch approaches.

SHAW. Oh, for god's sake, Richard, stop listening to everybody else! Be fearless! Follow your own goddamn star!

Shaw looks at Dreyfuss, a real attempt to get through to him.

"The wind passeth over us, and when we are gone the earth shall know us no more."

DREYFUSS. Are you okay?

SHAW. Oh, fuck you, Richard!

SFX: The launch bumps the boat.

Scheider appears.

They watch Roy carefully as he slowly enters the cabin.

(Aware of his condition.) Ahhh… How're you feeling, Roy?

SCHEIDER. Like a discarded sausage skin.

SHAW. A swig of this should help.

SCHEIDER. I'd rather have a glass of water.

SHAW. Remember what WC Fields said about water, Roy… You should avoid it. Fish fuck in it.

SCHEIDER. How appropriate.

SHAW. Go on.

SCHEIDER. Okay.

Scheider sits.

SHAW. Good man.

Shaw sits. Scheider sips and splutters like Dreyfuss.

SCHEIDER. Actually I think that has helped a little.

Dreyfuss enters and goes up to Shaw to move over so he can sit. Shaw closes his eyes nonchalantly and doesn't move. Drey-fuss decides to clamber under the table to sit in the middle.

SHAW. Big wrap party tonight?

DREYFUSS. Nah, Steven doesn't go for all that sentimental drunken crap…the hugging, the puking! Also I think he suspects that the crew are planning on throwing him in the drink after the final shot. My guess is he'll be straight out of Dodge before they get their hands on him.

SHAW. Clever fellow.

Beat.

DREYFUSS. I wonder if this'll be the one that breaks me, makes me a big shot. I thought it'd be *Duddy Kravitz* but, who knows, maybe it'll be this one.

SHAW. Don't fuckin' count your chickens! This thing hasn't been edited yet. You may well end up on the cutting room floor.

DREYFUSS. Yeah right. Like they're going to cut out the star!

SCHEIDER. "Star"?

SHAW. Oh, Christ!

DREYFUSS. With the caveat that you guys are both great, and I mean really great, supporting players, but let's be honest here—

SCHEIDER. Two things!—First, technically speaking, Brody is the hero of this film…and second, I dunno, maybe there isn't a star. Like I said before, maybe this is a new kind of movie.

Shaw pulls out a Jaws *poster mock-up.*

SHAW. Who gets top billing?

Dreyfuss snatches it to see.

SCHEIDER. Where the hell did this come from?

SHAW. My agent, John Gaines. It's all been approved.

DREYFUSS. Oh, my god, you fucked us! Your name's higher and in the middle!

SCHEIDER. Yeah, but I'm lower down on the left where people look next—or even first?

SHAW. No, no!

DREYFUSS. Well, I'm lower down and on the fucking right. Which is only good in countries where they read from right to left. I'm a star in the Middle East! My agent has screwed up again! Fucking Zanuck and Brown!

   Pause.

So, what are you guys doing after we wrap? Got anything lined up?

   Scheider gets up to get a drink and sits on the cooler.

SCHEIDER. Well, I'm reading the Goldman script. *Marathon Man*—you know, the Nazi thing? They've got Hoffman for the lead. They want me to play a Fed… Why am I always offered cops?

SHAW. It's your face, Roy. You've a look of incorruptibility.

SCHEIDER. Why thank you, Robert. So what's next for you two?

SHAW. For myself, I shall be getting the hell out of this benighted country and returning to Tourmakeady with my brood to concentrate on my writing. Back to the wet green grass and the smell of the peat fire!

SCHEIDER. So what about you, Richard?

DREYFUSS. Well, I tell you, I'm going to really double down on my career. Cut out the partying! It's time to get serious, do some theatre. Maybe Shakespeare. And Steven was telling me about this idea for a new movie he's got.

SCHEIDER. Oh yeah?

DREYFUSS. About UFOs.

SHAW. About what?

DREYFUSS. You know, flying saucers.

SCHEIDER. What, some *War of the Worlds*-type thing?

DREYFUSS. Uh, actually Steven sees the aliens as the good guys. Like they're trying to help mankind. You know, expand our consciousness.

SHAW. *(Sarcastic.)* Well that sounds like it's going to be good!

SCHEIDER. *(To Dreyfuss.)* Has Steven said he'll cast you?

DREYFUSS. I think he wants Nicholson, but he's impossible to work with, I'll wear him down.

SHAW. UFOs! Aliens! Jesus! Whatever next? Dinosaurs? Can this business get any more puerile?

DREYFUSS. Do you think they're gonna make a sequel?

SHAW. To what?

DREYFUSS. To this.

SHAW. Christ I hope not! Not much more to say is there?

SCHEIDER. One thing's for certain—if there is a sequel, I will not be in it.

DREYFUSS. Hey, never say never Roy.

SCHEIDER. What on earth could happen with Brody in a sequel? Another shark comes to town? That's crazy!

SHAW. Mark my words boys, one day there will only be sequels. Sequels and remakes, and sequels to remakes and remakes of sequels. Anyway, good luck to them bringing Quint back from the dead.

DREYFUSS. Oh, what? You think being bitten in half will stop them? They wouldn't even break a sweat! They'd just have Quint's never-before-mentioned twin brother show up.

SHAW. I'd sooner kill myself!

> *Shaw has a swig… Dreyfuss stares at the poster.*

DREYFUSS. What do you think it's about?

SCHEIDER. What?

DREYFUSS. *(Showing the poster.)* This movie. This fucking movie! It's got to be about something right? Everything's about something. I think it's about the subconscious.

SCHEIDER. Say again?

DREYFUSS. I mean, sharks are these ancient, primal creatures, right? So they represent the primal fear in all of us. All the terrors and desires we keep hidden—all that Freudian stuff my therapist's always talking about. That's what the shark is. You don't agree?

SCHEIDER. …It's an interesting theory…

DREYFUSS. So what do you think it's about?

SCHEIDER. I think it's about responsibility…when the government puts profit before people's lives, if you can't get rid of the bastards, you've gotta take care of the mess yourself—even if it terrifies you, for the good of the community.

DREYFUSS. Woah. Deep. What about you Robert, what do you think it's about?

SHAW. *It's about a shark!*

DREYFUSS. Yeah, but what's it really about?

SHAW. *It's really about a shark!!* Don't read any more into it. It's a thriller, a machine for making money. Do you really think people are going to be talking about this in fifty years?

> *SFX: Launch hits the boat hard. They all nearly lose balance.*

SCHEIDER. What the hell?

> *Scheider exits.*

DREYFUSS. Jesus, we've certainly run the gamut in this fucking boat over the last, what…nine weeks? Poker, gin rummy, spades, hearts, whist, slapjack, chicken foot, arm wrestling, pitch-and-toss—

SHAW. Shove ha'penny?

DREYFUSS. Fucking shove ha'penny!

SHAW. And tremendous fun it's been too.

> *Beat.*

DREYFUSS. I called Harold Pinter, by the way… I woke him up… He said he'd rather die.

> *Shaw laughs. Scheider reenters.*

SCHEIDER. Gentlemen, it delights me to be the bearer of good news. They are ready for our final shot.

> *They celebrate excitedly.*

SHAW. HOLY SHIT!

SCHEIDER. Incredible, isn't it?

SHAW. I feel like a prisoner on remand whose sentence has just been quashed!

DREYFUSS. Yesss! No more fucking chowder. No more Martha's Vineyard! And no sitting on this goddamn boat!

SCHEIDER. I gotta say, I feel kind of sad. It's been a pleasure, gentlemen.

DREYFUSS. Yeah, it's been a complete fucking nightmare!

SHAW. You know, if it wasn't for the vanity and the mannerisms you'd be a very good actor?!

DREYFUSS. You know, if it wasn't for the dullness and artistic pretension, you'd be a very good writer?! I might even read one of your books.

SHAW. You have to know how to read first, Richard.

> *They laugh.*

DREYFUSS. Bite me!

> *Dreyfuss clambers out and exits. When he reaches the window, he bangs it and sticks his tongue out at them.*

SHAW. Well done for keeping us alive, Roy.

SCHEIDER. I just want to say it's been an honor working with you.

SHAW. Thank you. You know, *(Quoting from* Casablanca.*)* "I'm no good at being noble, but it doesn't take much to see that the problems of three little people don't amount to a hill of beans in this crazy world."

SCHEIDER. "Here's looking at you, kid."

> *Scheider turns to leave.*

SHAW. Roy, you know that mass-extinction event you were talking about? I suspect one is coming for actors like you and me. I fear the future belongs to a generation of self-absorbed neurotics.

SCHEIDER. I think we'll be in good hands, Robert…

> *Scheider exits and climbs down into the launch…which then starts up and leaves.*
>
> *Shaw puts on his hat, takes the poster from the table and*

considers it…then moves to leave but stops in the cabin door-way. He pauses, wrestling in his mind. Then reaches back and picks up the half-drunk bottle of Lagavulin and leaves.

As the lights fade to black.

Scene 11—Indianapolis 3

They are placed for the reshoot of the Indianapolis speech.

ASSISTANT DIRECTOR. *(Voice-over.)* Okay, quiet please! Camera?

CAMERA OPERATOR. *(Voice-over.)* Rolling.

ASSISTANT DIRECTOR. *(Voice-over.)* Sound.

SOUND RECORDIST. *(Voice-over.)* Speed.

ASSISTANT DIRECTOR. *(Voice-over.)* Mark it.

FOCUS PULLER. *(Voice-over.)* Scene 191, D. Take two.

SFX: Clack.

SPIELBERG. *(Voice-over.)* Action!

SHAW. "Japanese submarine slammed two torpedoes into our side, chief. We was comin' back…from the island of Tinian to Leyte, we'd just delivered the bomb. The Hiroshima bomb. Eleven hundred men went into the water. Vessel went down in twelve minutes.

"Didn't see the first shark for about a half an hour. Tiger. Thirteen-footer. You know how you know that when you're in the water, chief? You tell by lookin' from the dorsal to the tail. What we didn't know, was our bomb mission had been so secret, no distress signal had been sent. Ha! They didn't even list us overdue for a week. Very first light, chief, sharks come cruisin', so we formed ourselves into tight groups.

SFX: Indianapolis music.

"Oh it was kinda like old squares in a battle, like you see in a calendar, like the Battle of Waterloo, and the idea was shark comes to the nearest man, that man he start poundin' and hollerin' and screamin' and sometimes that shark he go away…sometimes he wouldn't go away. Sometimes that shark he looks right into you. Right into your eyes. You know th' thing about a shark is he's got…lifeless eyes, black eyes, like a doll's eyes. When he comes at ya, he doesn't seem to be livin'…until he bites ya, and those black eyes roll over white and then…ah then you hear that terrible high-pitched screamin', the ocean turns red, and despite all the poundin' and the hollerin' they all come in and they…rip you to pieces.

"You know by the end of that first dawn, lost a hundred men. I don't know how many sharks, maybe a thousand. I don't know how many men, they averaged six an hour. On Thursday mornin', chief, I bumped into a friend of mine, Herbie Robinson from Cleveland. Baseball player. Boson's mate. I thought he was asleep. I reached over to wake him up. He bobbed up and down in the water, he was like a kinda top. Upended. Well, he'd been bitten in half below the waist. Noon the fifth day,

"Mr. Hooper, a Lockheed Ventura saw us. He swung in low and he saw us, young pilot, a lot younger than Mr. Hooper, anyway he saw us and come in low. And three hours later a big fat PBY comes down and start to pick us up. You know that was the time I was most frightened? Waitin' for my turn. I'll never put on a life jacket again. So, eleven hundred men went in the water, three hundred and sixteen men come out, the sharks took the rest, June the 29th, 1945… Anyway…we delivered the bomb."

SPIELBERG. *(Voice-over.)* Cut!

> *Blackout.*

End of Play

PROPERTY LIST

(Use this space to create props lists for your production.)

SOUND EFFECTS

(Use this space to create sound effects lists for your production.)

65

Hello, actors, theatre makers, and theatre fans,

On behalf of Broadway Licensing Global and the author*(s.)* of this work, we thank you for your continued support of the arts and the playwrights you love.

Like every title in our catalogue, this play is covered by copyright law, which ensures authors are rewarded for creating new dramatic work and protects them from theft and abuse of their work. We are compelled to impress upon all who obtain this edition that **this text may not be copied, distributed, or publicly produced in any way,** nor uploaded to any file-sharing websites or software—public or private. Any such action has an immediate and negative effect on the livelihood of the writer*(s.)*—it is also stealing and is against the law. As a result, should you copy, distribute, or publicly produce any part of this text without express written consent and licensed permission from our company—even if no one is being paid and/or admission is not being charged—your organization shall be subject to legal consequences that we are sure you want to avoid.

But we have faith in you and your understanding of these guidelines!

While this acting edition is the only approved text for performance, there may be other editions of the play available for sale. It is important to note that our team has worked with the playwright*(s.)* to ensure this published acting edition reflects their desired text for all future productions. If you have purchased a revised edition from us, that is the only edition you may use for performance, unless explicitly stated in writing by our team.

Finally, and this is an important one, **this script cannot be changed in any way** without written permission from our team. That said, feel free to reach out to us. We don't bite, and we are always happy to have a discussion to see if we can accommodate your request.

We are thrilled this play has made it into your hands and we hope you love it as much as we do. Thank you for helping us keep the theatre alive and well, and for supporting playwrights, in our continued journey to make everyone a theatre person!

Sincerely,
Fellow theatre lovers at Broadway Licensing Global

Note on Songs/Recordings, Images, or Other Production Design Elements

Be advised that Broadway Licensing neither holds the rights to nor grants permission to use any songs, recordings, images, or other design elements mentioned in the play. It is the responsibility of the producing theater/organization to obtain permission of the copyright owner(s.) for any such use. Additional royalty fees may apply for the right to use copyrighted materials.

For any songs/recordings, images, or other design elements mentioned in the play, works in the public domain may be substituted. It is the producing theater/organization's responsibility to ensure the substituted work is indeed in the public domain. Broadway Licensing cannot advise as to whether or not a song/arrangement/recording, image, or other design element is in the public domain.